A Book About My Uncle

A Child's Creation

Randi L. Millward

Instructions:

This book is a children's activity book. The sentences are started but left incomplete for the child to finish in his or her own words. The adjacent pages are intentionally left blank for the child to illustrate with his or her own personal artwork.

The artist may color with crayons, tape photos onto the paper, or use any other age-appropriate parent-approved artistic medium that does not bleed through the paper.

ISBN-10: 0989486532
ISBN-13: 978-0-9894865-3-8

More books by this author may be found online at
www.Amazon.com

A Book About My Uncle

By

____

Age: ______________

Date: ______________

My uncle is

____

____

____

______________________________________.

My uncle lives

____

____

____

______________________________.

I like when my uncle

____

____

____

____.

My uncle likes when I

____

____

____

______________________________________.

My uncle doesn't like

____

____

____

______________________________.

My uncle is really good at

____

____

____

______________________________.

My uncle says

____

____

____

____.

My uncle smiles when I

____

____

____

______________________________.

I have fun when my uncle and I

____

____

____

______________________________.

My uncle laughs when

____

____

____

____.

My favorite thing to do with my uncle is

____

____

____

____.

My favorite thing to play with my uncle is

____

____

____

______________________________.

I hope that someday my uncle

____

____

____

_______________________________________.

I get excited when my uncle

____

____

____

____.

When I am sad, my uncle

____

____

____

____.

My favorite thing about my uncle is

____

____

____

____.

I love my uncle because

____

____

____

____

______________________________________.

The End

www.ingramcontent.com/pod-product-compliance
Lightning Source LLC
LaVergne TN
LVHW010946110826
845149LV00013B/2774

* 9 7 8 0 9 8 9 4 8 6 5 3 8 *